Young People/
Tough Problems

Tova Navarra, R.N., B.A.

Young People/ Tough Problems

Tova Navarra, R.N., B.A.

Dedication
To Jim

All inquiries should be addressed to:
Barron's Educational Series, Inc.
250 Wireless Boulevard
Hauppauge, New York 11788
http://www.barronseduc.com

Library of Congress Catalog Card No.: 2002074376
International Standard Book No.: 0-7641-2067-0

Library of Congress Cataloging-in-Publication Data
Navarra, Tova.
    Young people/tough problems / Tova Navarra.
      p. cm.
    Summary: Provides guidance and encouragement for dealing with such
tough life issues as divorce, alcohol and drug addiction, depression, peer
pressure, dating, and guns in schools.
    ISBN 0-7641-2067-0
    1. Teenagers—Life skills guides—Juvenile literature. 2. Preteens—Life
skills guides—Juvenile literature. 3. Teenagers—Social conditions—
Juvenile literature. 4. Preteens—Social conditions—Juvenile literature.
5. Adolescent psychology—Juvenile literature. 6. Interpersonal relations
in adolescence—Juvenile literature. [1. Life skills. 2. Self-actualization
(Psychology) 3. Interpersonal relations. 4. Conduct of life.] I. Title.
HQ796.N367   2002
646.7'00835—dc21   2002074376

Contents

Author's Note To Young People

Dear You Who Are Wonderful But May Not Know It Yet:

As a young person in a complicated world, you have a lot to learn, think about, and do—especially as you grow into adulthood.

I have always believed you have personal power to get that job done well. You can think for yourself. You are capable of learning everything you need to know to achieve your goals. You have what it takes to be your own person and your own best friend. In fact, that's what this book is all about—a positive way to start figuring out how to deal with your issues in life.

Everyone has issues, or problems, of some kind. Life is devoted to making things work out, even when nothing seems to be going right. The way you choose to handle those problems can mean the difference between feeling horrible about what's happening to you and feeling great about yourself for overcoming the difficulties.

I say focus on your personal goals—what you really want to become—*and don't ever let anyone tell you you aren't smart, well adjusted, motivated, or good enough to accomplish them.* If you start out realizing how good you really are in plenty of ways, you'll have a head start. I wouldn't have written this book if I didn't know in my heart that you are terrific and that you have personal power you can use every day in every situation. As you read each part of this book, think about how you can apply the general idea of solving one problem you may *not* have to a problem you *do* have.

No matter who you are or where you come from, there's something for you in these pages. You may discover a good idea you never even thought about before. I wish I had all the answers, but of course I don't. But I encourage you to seek answers wherever life leads you. The real answers are mostly within you; you just have to reach deep inside to find them. Books such as this and people who care about you can be great sources of comfort and know-how. You simply need to open your mind, and be willing to see all the possibilities life has to offer. Remember that you're never stuck. Things can get better, because things are always changing. Help is there if you ask for it. Use all the gifts you were born with. I really believe in you— and I invite you to believe in yourself.

With love always,
Tova

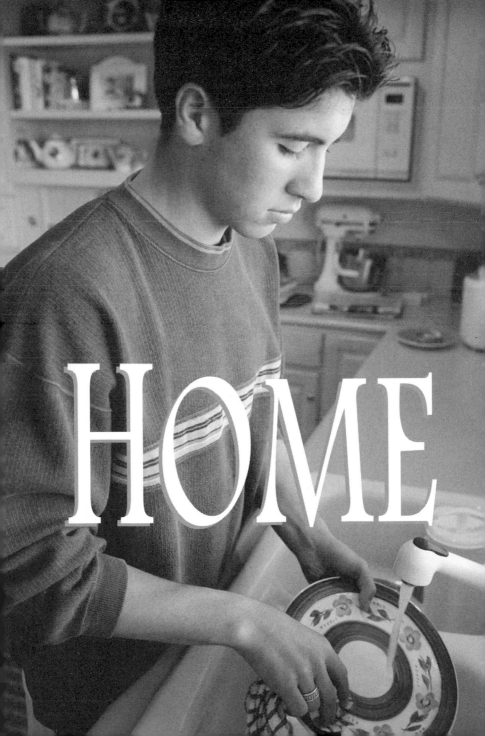

HOME

If your parents are getting a divorce,

you must realize that you are among many, many people your age in the same boat. Rampant divorce is a horrible testimony to difficult relationships in our culture, but it is so common that we have to deal with it. There are numerous causes for divorce—incompatibility (when people just don't get along well together), the desire for different lifestyles, money problems, lack of communication and intimacy, infidelity (when one or both parents find someone else to be romantically involved with), domestic violence and abuse, addiction,

mental illness or instability, and so on.

Kids, unfortunately, are often caught in the middle of their parents' battles. For the parents, divorce usually means relief from at least one problem, which is dealing on a daily basis with the offending spouse. For the kids, divorce means dividing up loyalties, dealing with the loss or lack of one parent's presence in the home, and perhaps having to deal with both Mom's and Dad's new friends and lifestyle. Yes, your preteen and teenage years will be affected by all this—*but* you are not alone, it is not your fault, and you will survive.

You will survive because you owe it to yourself to live your own life, no matter what your parents are doing with theirs. You have the right to feel sad, angry, and frustrated, but after you've allowed yourself to get through those feelings, you have your life ahead of you. You aren't always going to be as young as you are now. You're getting older and more independent, which is the normal route for each child. Don't bother thinking of yourself as stuck in your mother's or father's footsteps. That's a waste of your valuable time! Try to be as understanding as possible where your parents' heartaches are concerned, but start thinking of yourself as a unique individual, with talent, brains, and energy. Be realistic about doing well in school and moving yourself up the ladder of success. Your parents, divorced or together, can't chew your food for you! They're not going to call the shots on whether or not you succeed. That's up to you alone.

It's a good idea to talk about the divorce with both parents, if it's possible. For your own sake, tell them exactly how you feel and how you perceive what they're doing. They should know if you feel hurt, damaged, or confused, and they do have a responsibility to tell you the facts. Sometimes parents don't want to tell their kids everything that happened to cause the divorce, for fear of being blamed for wrongdoing or of causing the kids to resent the other parent for some reason. Let them know that you're old enough to get the idea that people make terrible mistakes and nobody's perfect. Let them know it may be harder for you to accept the divorce if you are left out of the explanation. However, one thing you may have to accept is their unwillingness to explain it to you. If this is the case, try to talk to someone you trust—for example, a counselor or school psychologist—about your feelings so they don't get all bottled up, and do your best to be good to yourself and think of your own goals in life. There are plenty of books you can read about children caught in the middle of divorce. You may be able to use some information that applies to you, or you may just need reassurance that divorce is a serious problem and there are ways of coping with it.

Your peers—that is, your friends and others in your own age-group—can be a big help, too, especially if they've experienced divorce in their families. Share your stories and feelings. Notice that they're all surviving to tell their stories! You might even find some things to laugh about together—you'd be surprised. No matter what's happening, life doesn't have to be all doom and gloom. Think of kids whose parents get divorced over and over. Forget about those marriages as a role model for you!

Try keeping a journal during and after the divorce. Writing down your feelings and observations can serve you well in the long run. You'll be able to see what you wrote in the beginning and how much things changed by your later entries. In other words, you'll see that you can cope, you can grow and learn from everything that's going on, and you may even be able to visualize how you'd like to set up your own life once you're completely independent of your parents.

Also, try to keep talking to both parents. It's important to maintain the lines of communication. They are your parents, after all, and both play a significant role in your life. Chances are they're concerned about your welfare and situation and they'll welcome the chance to be the best parent they can be to you. Parents and children really can learn a lot from each other if they choose to communicate and stay connected in a stable relationship.

If you're the child of a single parent and feel worried,

the first thing to do is talk openly with your parent about your concerns. Communication is powerful. It's worth it to speak up and be honest. A parent may not be aware that you're upset if you don't let them know. Moping around the house or staying in your room won't help whatever is bothering you. It's a relief for both you and your parent to discuss your life together, especially if you need to solve problems. Know that *parents* need to talk, also.

The second most important thing to do is realize that being a single parent can be difficult no matter how much your mom or your dad loves you. Parenting is one of the toughest jobs in the world, and there's no instruction book that "fits all." Each family is unique. Each parent and child has a unique relationship. It helps a lot if you both respect each other and give yourselves credit for doing your best. Did a friend ever tell you that you say or do a certain quirky thing, and you had no idea you were even doing it? This applies to being a parent: Sometimes Mom or Dad says a certain thing or acts a certain way and isn't aware of how it affects you. Again, talking things out may be the best start.

Sometimes it helps to think of your single parent as a sort of juggler—a high-energy performer who has to earn a living (which may mean having more than one job), manage a household, maintain a social life, and take care of you. It's like having several flaming torches to juggle all at once, all the time. NOT EASY. And you have responsibilities, too. You have to juggle your home life (which means doing your

share to make life easier for everyone), your school life, and your social life. None of these things is a snap. With everyone constantly juggling, life can seem like a circus that never ends and may not be loads of fun all the time. People get tired and stressed, and they often take it out on each other. It happens to the best of us: Your parent gets short-tempered with you, and you criticize him or her for not being a "storybook" mom or dad. Perhaps you feel angry that you don't have two parents. Maybe you hate that your mom has to work so hard, or that your dad is dating someone you don't like. Maybe you're just ticked off because you're feeling lonely or bored. Imagine how your parent feels at times.

If you're in this kind of cycle of behavior, stop and think. Come forward and tell your parent honestly what's bugging you *once you really know what it is* (or even if you're not sure). Don't confuse Mom's forgetting to bring home pizza with your *really* being upset because you wanted to spend some time with her. It's not about the pizza. It's about your relationship. If you can identify the source of your feelings deep down, you'll avoid having fights about the wrong things. If you have what you think are complicated and disturbing issues that you can't go directly to your parent about, ask your guidance counselor, a teacher you like, a coach, or another trustworthy adult what you can do. Some issues pose truly painful problems, such as those in other parts of this book. Remember, even smart and caring adults need to talk to someone about their problems at times. Reading self-help books that pertain to your particular problems can also be a great help and comfort. We're all here on earth to help each other one way or another. Help others—and you'll help yourself!

EVERYONE NEEDS HELP FROM TIME TO TIME. Everyone reaches a point in his or her life when nothing seems to be going right, or when situations cause sorrow, depression, disgust, anger, fear, or frustration. Try to keep in mind that everyone runs into difficulties. The challenge is moving beyond them. Remember: we're supposed to be strong, decent human beings who get through hard times. We're meant to learn from our problems and mistakes in order to move on and move up in life. So, kick your dignity and integrity into gear. Think about what you need to be happy and well adjusted. Ask yourself what it will take to fix some of the things that bother you. Tell your parent what you think. Express yourself, but don't be put off by your parent's reaction. He or she is not perfect. *Be a partner* with your parent (or whomever you trust) in creating solutions. Change often comes about when people put their heads together and work things out. You deserve the best, and very often, you can *make* the best of anything if you're willing to try.

If you're having trouble with a stepparent,

you may feel your whole life is a mess or out of control. This is because you may be grieving. Many young people in your situation do not realize they are in a state of grief—that is, the way you feel when someone you love dies or a tragedy or great loss occurs. You could be grieving the loss of your original family. You may be extremely sad that your father and mother aren't married to each other anymore. You may deeply resent that your parents are not going to get back together again, especially after one or both remarries. Or you may be suffering because one parent has died. You may feel that no one on the face of the earth could ever replace that parent, which is a normal feeling and part of the grieving you're going through. You may dislike your stepparent and wonder how your mother or father could have picked this person to live with. Or you may like your stepparent but feel guilty and disloyal to the parent who is no longer living with you. These things can give you plenty of grief.

Grief is a powerful emotion. The first thing to do is realize that about half of all married couples in America get divorced—not a pretty scene. But give yourself a break. Find quiet time alone and tell yourself you have suffered a real loss. Allow yourself to feel bad, but, as much as it hurts, allow yourself to know you will feel better in time. Eventually, you'll feel like yourself again. Healing emotionally from loss or other trouble takes time, so give yourself lots of time as though it were a birthday present. You might want to say to yourself, "My feelings of grief are normal, and I allow myself to get better each day."

Now try to imagine that you're in a play, playing the part of a loving parent. You need to be kind, patient, gentle, and smart, just the way you'd like parents to be. You have to memorize your lines, like telling yourself you'll be all right and you can work things out. Ask yourself what you need to do for yourself right now. Make a plan. In the role of your own parent, love yourself enough to say that deep down, your life can be everything you want it to be. This doesn't mean your actual parents aren't necessary or important in your life—they most certainly are. But sometimes we need to give ourselves some comfort and confidence.

Another thing you might do is find a classmate or other person who lives with a stepparent. Together you can talk about your problems and let off a lot of steam, because each of you knows how it really feels to be in this situation. Help and support each other. That can be an enormous comfort.

Because you probably did not have a choice in your parents' decision to get a divorce and live with different people, you may feel frustrated. You may take your frustration out on the new stepparent, your real parent, someone else, or yourself. If you and your stepparent are having a hard time getting along, stick up for yourself. Express your feelings openly *without throwing a tantrum or calling names*. Try to explain the difficulty you are facing to both your parent and stepparent. They may surprise you and really help things get on a better track.

If they don't seem to understand or do not want to listen, talk to an adult you trust, such as a good friend's parent, the school nurse, a teacher, school psychologist, or guidance counselor. These people can listen to your problems without judging them or you. They may offer suggestions that can help. Keep trying to get through. No matter how tangled up things become, communication is the most important way to start solving problems. Communicate with yourself, too, because talking to yourself helps you calm down, be honest about your own feelings, and make a reasonable plan for smoothing things out. It may sound crazy, but lots of answers to your questions are already within you. Set them free, and listen to what your heart tells you. If your parents won't listen to your point of view, maybe it's because you become obnoxious or difficult and block the progress of communication. Consider your approach! No one wants to deal with an angry grizzly bear.

Getting along with a stepparent's children may also pose problems for you. Perhaps you feel slighted or left out, and believe that the other kids are favored. If you are the oldest, the younger ones may seem to get all the attention, or you may suddenly be given the responsibility of watching them or taking care of them. You may find you have more chores to do because of the new kids. Maybe they really bug you, get into your things, and make nuisances of themselves. If you are the youngest, the other kids may tease or bully you. You may notice your biological parent being supernice to your stepparent's kids and feel hurt or betrayed.

Lots of problems can arise when a stepparent brings other young people into your household. Here again, you have to stick up for yourself without starting fights, acting wild, or behaving badly. Teach yourself to take several deep breaths in and out when you feel stressed by others. That can "center" you, calm you down, and help you keep your head on straight about all of this, because time passes faster than you think. You won't live with the situation forever. You'll grow up, go to college, or get a job and move out of your parents' home. Once you are older, you can make your own decision about the relationship you'll have with your stepparent's kids.

Besides speaking up when you have a problem or feel bad about something, try to find ways to be a friend to the other young person or persons. Remember that they are also in the position of suddenly having to live and get along with *you*. Nobody has it easy. Showing kindness makes a great difference in how you live your daily life.

If you don't want to continue fighting and having problems, talk things over with the other kids, if that's possible. If you all get on the same side, life may take a surprising turn for the better. On the other hand, if the kids refuse to be kind and decent with you, keep to yourself as much as you can. When you cannot be by yourself and the others insist on bugging you, try your hand at being patient. Understand that younger kids aren't as sophisticated as you are. Set a good example for them. Avoid getting hooked into a fight. Get involved in activities you like, and apply the Golden Rule: Treat others the way you want them to treat you. This goes for your stepparent, too. You may not like the person, but if you can at least be kind to him or her, you'll be better off for it and you'll feel better about yourself.

If your stepparent is abusive, that's another story. NO ONE HAS THE RIGHT TO ABUSE ANOTHER PERSON. Speak up loudly and do so until your parent or another adult you trust helps you. Your parent may not know or may deny that the stepparent is doing anything he or she should not be doing. Do not allow the stepparent to undermine your self-esteem, hit you, or touch you in a way you do not want to be touched. *People who physically or sexually abuse their stepchildren are committing a crime.* There are agencies in your community you can call if you are being abused in any way. Ask the school nurse, a teacher, a leader in your house of worship, or someone who cares about you how to get in touch with an agency that will investigate your situation and help you find relief as soon as possible.

Remember that life with stepparents and stepsiblings isn't always like life with *The Brady Bunch*. Be realistic. Life can be difficult, but you *can* succeed. Do your best to take care of yourself while knowing your parents need to live their own lives, too. Their choices may not be ones you'd make, but try to respect the fact that nobody is perfect and that no one can tell another person whom to love or marry. Sometimes you just have to think of whatever happens as the way things are meant to be, even if you can't know why.

If you're a foster child and feel unhappy,

first stop and think hard about your situation. Ask yourself the right questions: What exactly is making me feel bad? Are my foster parents mean to me? Do they cause me physical or emotional pain? If so, how do they do that? If not and they're basically OK, am I feeling blue because I'm not with my biological parents? Am I angry with them? Am I having trouble in school? Do I feel that I'm not as good as other kids who are not living in a foster home? What really, deep down, is my problem?

The most important thing to remember is that *no one has the right to abuse you in any way.* If you are being beaten, threatened, deprived of food, or forced to do things you know are wrong, you have the right to tell people who can help you—your teacher, your friend's mom, the school principal, the school nurse, a child-abuse hotline worker, anyone who will take you seriously. It's very important to protect yourself, *even if you feel afraid to do so.* Find someone who will call a social worker or person who can change your situation for the better.

If your home life is all right, maybe you feel unhappy for other reasons. Sometimes foster kids feel they just don't fit in with the family. Sometimes a foster home is one in which several foster children live and it's hard to get along with everyone or have privacy. You may have a deep desire to know your biological parents, and this frustrates you or makes you feel disloyal toward your foster family. You might have just arrived in your new home and everything seems odd or "foreign" to you. Or you may be having trouble connecting with your foster parents, especially on touchy subjects like having a foster parent who has an alcohol or drug abuse problem or having to share a room with another child who may be doing something wrong. What would have to happen in order to change your bad feelings and get you into a more comfortable way of life?

You almost have to be your own lawyer and find someone who will help you make those changes. Remember: Change is possible. Problems may be easier to solve than you think. Perhaps all you have to do to have more privacy around the house is talk to your foster mom about it. She may be able to arrange a better situation for you. Maybe you can talk to your foster dad about getting some help with homework, and he can settle that situation. The most important thing for you to do is know you're good enough and strong enough to solve problems. Be patient, and be willing to come from love, not anger. If you go raging at your caregivers like a mad bull, their natural response may be to get angry back or pull away from you. Instead, approach them when you have a cool head and a fairly calm way of expressing your problem. Understand that most people who want foster kids are the kind of people who come from love. They're giving a lot even though they may not have a lot for themselves. They want to help. So give them—and your situation with them—a chance. There may even be a situation in which you will have to think of a solution for yourself and actually work it out with the others, parents and kids. Be a person who thinks things through and who can compromise. *Life is never perfect.* Learning to figure things out for yourself is a wonderful skill that will make you stronger and set an example for those around you.

If a loved one in the household is seriously ill,

you may feel very frustrated about a lot of things. You may not be able to play in certain areas where the sick person is, or you may not be able to turn up your music loud or watch TV when you'd like. You may not be able to go on family trips, and you may not be allowed to have friends in or be at a friend's house for very long. Caring for one who is very sick means changes for everyone. These changes may be hard on the whole family.

The family goal here is to give the best care to the sick person so that he or she can get well. That may take a long time and lots of patience. Sometimes the ill person is not expected to recover, which is extremely difficult to cope with both physically and emotionally. Knowing that someone you love will probably die makes family life very different. You may feel that a cloud of darkness looms over everything. You may feel scared, sad, angry, or helpless. It's often hard to be considerate and quiet. It may even be difficult for you to help care for the sick person.

The best thing to do is keep up your grades in school, and let teachers know how things are going at home. Ask for some understanding, but don't let the situation ruin your life. The person who is sick would not feel better knowing you were letting everything that's important to you slide down the drain. Do your best to cooperate with the family. You'll feel strong and good about yourself if you cooperate. Remember that the situation won't last forever, and there is hope for things to get back to a normal routine.

Talk to an adult you trust about your feelings. Don't set yourself apart from your friends. Talk to them, too, and participate in as many activities as you can. Perhaps your parents and your friends' parents can get together and figure out ways for you to have a social life, like having a pizza party at a friends' house or carpooling with your friends to the movies, with each family sharing either some of the tasks or expenses. There's no need to feel guilty about having a good time. Socializing is one of the most important things in life. It makes you feel connected and helps you develop interpersonal skills.

You can also talk to the one who is sick, if that's possible. Be honest and say what's really on your mind. It's okay to let that person know you feel sad or confused or mad. He or she might be feeling the same way, and you can share your thoughts. Think what a relief that could be! Good communication can help in so many ways, and it's often the simplest solution. Another good thing is to do kind things for the ill person. Not only will it make the person feel good, it will always be a good personal memory for you.

If you have a parent who has an alcohol or drug addiction,

please know that it is not your fault, and it is not your responsibility to "take care" of that parent. Another important thing to remember is that abusing drugs or alcohol causes many other horrible problems and IT IS NEVER A SOLUTION TO ANYTHING. Addicts are not people to admire and emulate.

Addiction to any substance—alcohol or drugs—is a serious problem that requires help from doctors and counselors. Alcoholics

Anonymous (AA) and Narcotics Anonymous (NA) are two organizations that offer help to both the addict and the addict's family. Al-Anon and Alateen are groups specifically designed to help those whose lives are affected by someone else's drinking. Look up their numbers in your local phone book, or log onto their web sites, and then contact them to see what you can do to improve your life at home.

Also, remember that alcoholism is a disease, and drug addiction may indicate severe emotional problems. Being ashamed is unnecessary and doesn't help! Don't let insults people may hurl at you or your family bother you. They're not worth anything, and they come from fear and stupidity!

You do have the right to feel sad and angry that things are not good at home because of addiction. You are normal if you have feelings of resentment that in turn make you feel guilty for having them. Addiction creates major difficulties and hardships. Focus on the fact that you are not alone with your problem. Many young people are trying to cope with the same thing. The key is being willing to talk about the problem and ask for help from the right sources.

Be willing to speak up to family members about the situation. You may want to talk to a social service agency (ask your teacher, principal, or guidance counselor how to contact the appropriate agency) to get help. Keeping a "family secret" is useless. Suffering in silence doesn't get you anywhere. Find out all you can about alcoholism or addiction from books or the Internet. Reading about the problem may give you a better handle on how to deal with your particular situation.

In general, no matter what your problem may be, reach for the stars. Go for the gold. Did you ever hear the old expression, "The squeaky wheel gets the grease"? Don't be afraid to squeak! Babies cry when they're hungry. Dogs bark when something is wrong. Sick people go to the doctor. Getting good help means you have to be proactive, which means you have to get the ball rolling by your *action*. It's good to be proactive, especially because it involves preventing more or worse problems in the future—and prevention is precious.

If a loved one can't or won't quit smoking,

you probably wish you had a magic wand to make him or her stop. You feel troubled by the fact that smoking causes lung disease, which can be fatal. At times, you wonder why your loved one doesn't seem to care that smoking is so dangerous, and your anger wells up. You think: How could someone be so stupid? Doesn't he or she care what can happen to all of us? If everyone knows smoking is bad, why do so many people still do it?

First, try to learn all you can about addiction to nicotine. That's the drug in cigarettes and tobacco that starts all the trouble. Once a person is addicted, he or she craves nicotine so strongly that it's very difficult to quit. People often say nicotine relaxes them or they enjoy the effect of it, but that's because they've trained their bodies to *need* nicotine in order to feel right. Quitting means retraining their bodies to not need it, and that is a real challenge. Read up on the problem and get to know what kind of help is available for smokers.

Let the person know exactly how you feel about his or her smoking habit and the bad effects smoke can have as it floats through the house and into other people's lungs. Ask if there's any way you can help. Tell the person you know about nicotine patches and gum and programs to help people quit, and say how important it is to you that he or she quits. You may want to get a protective mask for yourself (they look like the ones surgeons wear during an operation) so you don't have to breathe in all that secondhand smoke. Wearing a mask in the house may send a strong message to the smoker.

Understand, too, that although some people are willing to work very hard to stop smoking, others won't stop no matter what anyone says or does. Some people won't even stop after they have lung cancer! Unfortunately, you have to live with whatever that person chooses for himself or herself. You can't control anyone but yourself. If you are faced with a person who will not stop smoking, the best you can do is put your anger aside and focus on keeping up your own life and health. Use this bad example as a way to remind yourself not to smoke or be self-destructive in any way. Tell your friends how awful smoking is and how they should avoid it.

If your parents leave you alone a lot,

you may feel angry and left out or that you have too much responsibility in their absence. Consider the reasons they leave you alone: Is it because they each have demanding jobs with long hours? Is it because they are always going out with their friends? Is it because they belong to a club or organization that requires their time after work? Find out the real reason, if you can. Talk to your parents honestly about the situation. Let them know that it makes you feel bad or uneasy, and ask what can be done to solve the problem. If your parents need to leave you alone because of their work, they may have no choice, and they may hate the idea that you're alone. However, they may be able to help the situation by getting you into a fun program or finding a companion for you or someplace nice for you to stay until they get home. Perhaps you can even join them for a short time in their workplace.

You have a right to speak up about your problem. Tell your parents how you feel about being left alone so much. Ask them to help ease the situation for you.

If for some reason you have to cope with being alone, use the time to do good things for yourself. Think of fun things you can do. You can watch movies or play video games without someone telling you to stop. You can put on music and sing at the top of your lungs. You can dance all around the house with no one there, and you can do all sorts of pretend activities, like pretending you are skiing down a mountain or hosting your own talk show. Time alone may not always be a negative thing. Lots of people

wish for some "peace and quiet" or time to themselves, because our lives, in general, are always so busy. Writers, sculptors, painters, and many others enjoy uninterrupted time to themselves so they can be creative. Try it!

If your parents won't let you go out with friends,

talk to them about the situation. Be honest. Most young people are allowed to go to their friends' homes or on outings with their friends' families. Sleepovers are popular, too, as are parties given by friends whose parents are home to supervise, and school activities that involve overnight or day trips. All this is part of learning to get along with people and enjoying social activities.

Your parents are most likely saying no

because they are worried you may want to hang out with people who aren't supervised by parents or teachers or who seem to be troubled. They want to protect you; that's their right and obligation. Your parents have the right to limit your contact with anyone who is too wild or interested in inappropriate activities. Be grateful that your parents care about you so much. It could be a serious problem, however, if your parents *never* want you to socialize, which is not considered normal, and you need to talk with them and someone who can counsel you and your family.

One solution may be to have a friend or two come to your house so they can get to know your family. Have their parents talk with your parents. Maybe the families can coordinate a pizza party, a trip to the movies, or a sleepover that won't make anyone worry you may not be safe. Choose your friends wisely, and you'll usually have a great time.

HEALTH

If you're being physically or sexually abused,

get in touch with your local police department, tell them what the problem is, and ask for a hotline number you can call. There are services that help protect young people from abusive situations, and YOU DESERVE TO BE SAFE. Don't wait to call for help. Don't be ashamed or feel guilty. Remember: No one has the right to hurt you—not your mother, father, sister, brother, aunt, uncle, cousin, neighbor—NO ONE.

Never think it's your own fault, either.

People who abuse others are committing a crime. You must not "protect" them or "keep their secret." It's just plain horrible to take abuse and not tell.

If you are being threatened or abused, write down how, when, and where it happened. Tell any adult you trust at school, at your house of worship, or in your community that you need help. *Keep talking to people about your situation until someone listens and takes you seriously.* That's very important. The school nurse can help. Every community has some sort of agency that offers help in this kind of situation. Use your personal power! It's no disgrace that you can't handle this on your own. It's too difficult, and you deserve to be protected. Be strong enough to help yourself and help stop bad things that are going on. Your life can change. You can be the one who changes it.

If you have a disability and feel inferior or deprived,

you need to go deep down in your heart and find strength and love there. We're all on our own special mission in life. Some of us are so-called normal, and some of us are different, perhaps with challenges that seem very difficult, painful, or unfair. The most important thing for you to remember and say to yourself every day is that you are on your mission, and your mission is valuable. Get to know about other people in the world who had to overcome a great challenge. Think of people such as Helen Keller, who struggled with being blind, deaf, and unable to speak when she was young but who became one of the most educated and beloved women in history. There are athletes, singers, actors, musicians, teachers, doctors, and people in all walks of life who pushed past their disabilities to become the best they could be. Find out about them. They're your inspiration.

You say those people just got a lucky break, or they didn't have it as hard as you do? Maybe so, but the one thing they all share is the ability to figure out what they liked to do best and what they could do best. Then they took this skill as far as they could until other people couldn't help but notice how well they were doing. Parents, teachers, and caregivers can tell you to believe in yourself until the cows come home, but if you don't tell yourself you can have a great life, no one can tell you anything. *You can have a great life*. You are responsible for creating a great life for yourself. Think about it and get real. What skills do you already have? List them and say thank you for each one. What

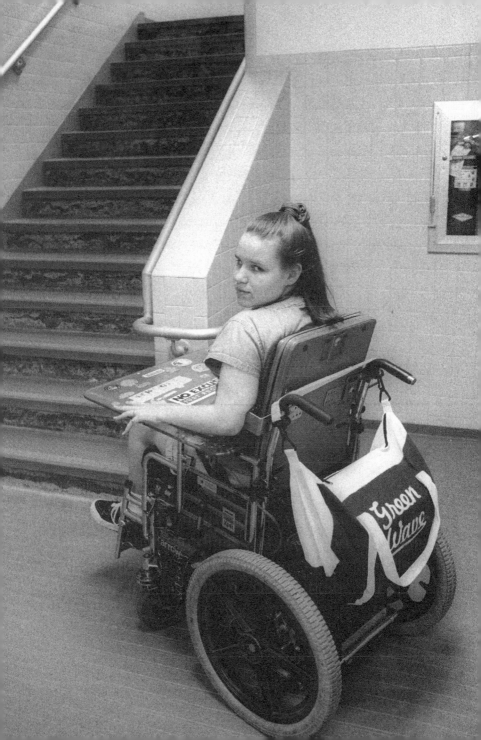

do you want to learn about or do? Once you know what kind of activity makes you feel really happy, ask your caregivers how you can get to do it. They'll be delighted to help. Remember, be realistic, but never lose the "do the impossible" motivation, either. Some may tell you that you'll never achieve your goal, but THERE ARE MANY WAYS TO SUCCEED, and you can find one of those ways.

Ask for the help you need. Talk to the people who care about you. Let them know what's on your mind. Also, find out about organizations and support groups that can help with your specific challenge. They're available on the Internet and their phone numbers and addresses are available at your local medical center.

If you have a weight or other physical problem,

you're most likely feeling bad about yourself. You may be too heavy or too thin, you may have acne, or you may need braces—and what you really want is to be "normal." Young people are very concerned with body image, or self-image. How you look can mean everything to you a lot of the time. Others judge you, and if you're out of the average weight or have problem skin, they may reject you or make fun of you. That's never an easy thing to deal with, but you can do something about it. There are treatments for acne and many other conditions. Ask to be taken to your family physician to see what can be done for you.

You can also help yourself in many ways. For example, many people who are overweight eat more food than their bodies really need. They eat for fun, not because they're hungry. They may think food is a substitute for love or a reward for being good, which actually is harmful. Being fat takes a toll on your heart, lungs, liver, and other important organs. Also, you can't move quickly or easily, and clothes are a problem. Worst of all, you're not happy with the way you look. Everyone wants to look his or her best. The good news is you can change your eating habits and lose weight. First you must be willing to work hard at it. Don't get lazy and discouraged. Losing weight takes time, patience, and strength of character. The best news is YOU CAN REALLY DO IT IF YOU WANT TO.

Think of what you eat every day. What foods do you eat that are fattening? Burgers and fries? Pepperoni pizza? Chips? Shakes? Make a list of them and decide to eat them less often and in smaller portions. Replace them with foods that are more nutritious and are not as fattening. Ask for help with this. Talk to your parents, a teacher, the school nurse, or your doctor. A good diet doesn't mean you have to starve yourself or never have your favorite foods. Have an adult who cares about you and knows something about nutrition help you set up a new eating plan. Learn about the food pyramid. This chart, which is shaped like a pyramid, comes from the federal government to guide your food intake. It shows which foods are most beneficial to you. On the very top of

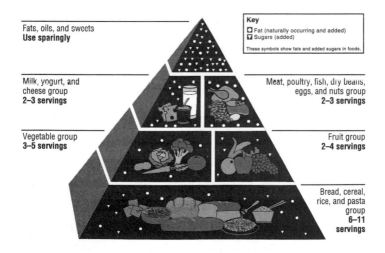

Key
☐ Fat (naturally occurring and added)
☑ Sugars (added)
These symbols show fats and added sugars in foods.

Fats, oils, and sweets
Use sparingly

Milk, yogurt, and cheese group
2–3 servings

Meat, poultry, fish, dry beans, eggs, and nuts group
2–3 servings

Vegetable group
3–5 servings

Fruit group
2–4 servings

Bread, cereal, rice, and pasta group
6–11 servings

the pyramid—the smallest space—are sugars and fats. Eat the least amount of them as a rule, but *sometimes* it's fine to have a dessert or special food you like. All you need to do is balance healthier foods with the junk or other fun (and unhealthier) food.

Taking these steps makes sense if you want to lose weight. Also, you must find a good way to exercise to help burn any excess calories you get from food—that is, calories your body doesn't need to perform its daily functions. Walking is the easiest exercise and doesn't require special equipment. Ask your school nurse or doctor about the best exercise program for you. Steer clear of "miracle diets" or other commercial diet products that may be unhealthy for you. *Eating less and exercising are the only real ways to lose weight, because they change your daily behavior.* As you teach your body to require less food and respond to more exercise, your body will modify itself to a better weight and energy level.

Also, stay in touch with reality. You may never be really thin because that simply may not be your body type. Just remember that thinner doesn't always mean better. By changing the way you eat and becoming more active, you can feel a whole lot better about yourself.

Gaining weight if you are too thin may also be a challenge. Depending on your body type, it may not be healthy to be very thin, and your energy level may be too low. Like people who are overweight, you also have to eat the right foods according to the food pyramid. Loading up exclusively on sugar and fat is unhealthy. Everyone needs a balanced diet—that is, the right amount of protein, carbohydrates, and other nutrients—in order to function normally. You also need the right amount of exercise. Consult your school nurse or your family doctor for good, personalized advice.

If you are slim *but you have a terrible fear of getting fat or if you actually see yourself as fat*, you may not be eating enough to sustain your health. You may even have decided not to eat most of the time. Talk to your parents immediately about this. You may have an eating disorder called anorexia. Although it can dangerous, effective treatments are available. Young girls are more likely to have the disorder, probably because our culture encourages us to believe you have to be thin to be beautiful. But anorexia and other eating disorders can be prevented if they are recognized right away. Don't hesitate to help yourself, and don't be ashamed. Help is out there for you. Remember: You are a beautiful person from the inside out, so be good to yourself. Always come from love, not fear.

If you feel sad or depressed for long periods of time,

you need to get to the bottom of the trouble. Everyone feels sad and depressed at times, but these feelings go away and life goes on as usual. On the other hand, people who are *always* sad or depressed may have a serious problem that requires professional help. If you've felt down in the dumps for weeks and weeks, even months, do a good thing for yourself right now—talk to someone you feel close to about it. Whether the problem is big or small doesn't

matter. If it's getting to you in a bad way, it's worth talking about it. What if you don't know what's really bothering you? All the more reason to keep talking until something comes out. You *do* know what's wrong deep down. *You're the only one who really knows.* You just need to make yourself aware of it.

Maybe talking to yourself when you're alone can help. When no one else is around, tell yourself about your problem. Go on and on, giving all the details. You might want to write things down as you talk, and add to your notes whenever you think you've touched on something significant. Keep a diary. Listen to yourself. Tell yourself what it would take to make you feel better about life. Tell yourself what you really want, what would make you truly happy. Let yourself fantasize about those things and feel good in the moment of thinking about them. Remind yourself that daydreaming or concentrating on something that would make you happy is one way to set your goals. It's a way to focus on the positive and tell yourself you deserve good things in life. Talk about everything that's already good for you. Talk about the things you want to change. Don't hold out—allow yourself to be open and honest with you!

Some signs of depression are sleeping too much or not being able to sleep much, loss of appetite or overeating, lack of interest in things you'd usually enjoy, and hiding away alone in your room for too much of the time.

If you can talk to yourself, you can also talk to someone who can counsel you. Don't think you can't stop being sad or blue. Depression is common, and it's curable. Be proactive. That means ask for help and be willing to make changes. Don't be embarrassed to see a doctor. Feeling well emotionally is important every single day. Why muddle through when you can enjoy and feel comfortable?

SCHOOL

If you feel overwhelmed and stressed by school,

first remember that you are very smart. If you weren't, you wouldn't be reading this book! Then remind yourself that each person in the world has certain abilities and certain short-comings. You may be great at math but average in English. You may have a real talent for play-ing the drums or the piano, or you may excel in a sport. You may be a total geek in a cooking class but wonderful at mechanical drawing or car engine repair. Many people have several talents, but some just don't realize how much talent they really have. Are you one of them? If you're feeling stressed out by school, then you just may be one of those people.

Try to figure out the real reason you're feeling overwhelmed and stressed. Is the actual work too much or too fast for you? Are you involved in too many activities? Do you have a hectic home life? Is there too much competition? Where exactly is the pressure coming from? Talk to yourself, and then talk to your parents. Try to get the feelings into words so you can look over the whole situation as clearly as possible.

If you see what the problem really is, then talk it over with an adult who cares about you. Figure out what can be done to ease up on things. Perhaps you'll have to cut some of the less important stuff out of the picture, or perhaps you need more time to finish your homework. Most of the time, there's a solution to the problem.

If you don't get to the heart of the matter and you still feel overwhelmed, look at the effects of that feeling. If you are so stressed that you feel sick to your stomach all the time, you may need to talk to your doctor or a psychologist. If you feel so overwhelmed by everything that you feel almost paralyzed, you shouldn't try to muddle through on your own. Ask for help. Many people have the same problem. Help is available, so why not be good to yourself and get some?

If your problem stems from schoolwork that seems too hard, talk to your teachers about what you can do. Let them know you're having trouble. Show them you're willing to help yourself—they'll be impressed by that. Keep in mind that there may be a simple solution to your problem. Perhaps a teacher will offer to help you after school, give you different tasks to do, or help you ask questions when you're feeling confused.

If you're worried about someone bringing a gun or other weapon to school,

you should give yourself credit for being a sensitive person. It is a terrible situation when a young person has access to a gun and decides to put himself or herself and others in danger. School violence has caused tragic results. No one has the right to create an unsafe environment for others.

But worrying about it doesn't really help. It's better if you turn worry into action and report anyone you think or know has a gun to

your teacher or another person in authority at the school. *Report it immediately.* There's no sense in waiting. A tragedy can occur in a split second. Unfortunately, some young people are so angry, frustrated, or mentally imbalanced that they feel they need a weapon as a show of strength. What they don't realize is that violence doesn't equal strength. Violence won't solve their emotional problems.

It is also unfortunate that so many of the TV shows and movies we all watch contain terrible violence. This can have a bad effect on some people. They may be overly influenced by the violence, or they may think it's exciting and fun. That's how the moviemakers present it. It looks glamorous. In fact, some people may forget altogether that these are just shows. In reality, violence means injury, destruction, loss, and the worst kind of heartache and pain.

Smart, sensitive people like you know the difference between what comes out of Hollywood and what is real life. Limit the number of violent shows you watch, and always remind yourself that what seems thrilling on the screen is NOT THE WAY TO DEAL WITH REAL LIFE.

It's okay to let teachers and school administrators know you are concerned about the gun issue. Part of their job is to see that students are as safe as possible during school hours. Talk about your concerns to your family, too, particularly if you know of a student who has bragged about having a gun or said he or she would open fire (or do some sort of harm) at school.

DO NOT STAY IN ANYONE'S HOME OR IN ANY OTHER PLACE WHERE THERE ARE GUNS. The potential for an accident is too great to take a chance. Young people should never think a gun is a toy or an amusement. Guns are deadly weapons, and *you can never be sure a gun is not loaded.* Although many people believe owning guns serves a purpose, others believe having guns leads to violence and unnecessary death. If a friend wants to show you a gun or wants you to participate in some game involving a gun, leave right away. Arguing with him or her may lead to a fight. Just protect yourself and quickly get home. Let your family know that your friend has access to a gun, even if he or she has never played with or used a gun. Prevention can make a life-or-death difference.

If you encounter a bully or a gang of bullies,

you need to report any dangerous behavior to the school authorities, the local police, and your parents. You have the right to be safe. It is not a sign that you are weak or a wimp. No one should threaten or try to hurt you physically. No one should take your lunch, your money, or your belongings. What's more, no one who does such a thing should get away with it. If someone starts to bully you or threaten you, go quickly into a store or place of business if you can, and tell an adult what is going on. Ask for help. Try not to hang out in isolated areas where you have no protection. Stay in areas where other people are around. Avoid anyone you think might mean trouble.

A bully is usually a person who has very low self-esteem, and the only way he or she can feel tough is to pick on others. In a gang, a bully feels even tougher, because the gang is sort of like a family that sticks together. In this "family," the bully feels protected and secure, so in front of them he acts meaner or stronger than he really is. There is no reason to take any abuse from a bully and his gang. Don't try to get around them—because actually you may not be able to—and don't let them beat you up or somehow get the better of you. REPORT THEM. You'll protect not only yourself but others, too. Most important, you may help prevent someone from actually getting hurt.

SOCIAL

If you feel you have less than others,

first tell yourself that the finest things in life begin in your heart and mind. You are intelligent; you have the potential to become anything you want to be in your life. No one can take your natural talents and gifts away from you. As a young person in the household, you may feel that the lack of money means a lack of good character or worth. That's not necessarily true. Parents who don't make a lot of money may be working as hard as they can and feel very frustrated, just the way you do when you can't have certain things that others may have.

Seeing other kids who have a lot of nice things, such as designer clothes and various luxuries, may stir feelings of jealousy or resentment in you. You may wish you had those things, too, but remember that most of us want certain material comforts. Most adults would rather have nice things than not have anything, too. Our society teaches us that having things is better and that attaining these things should be one of our goals in life. Your feelings are not because you're a bad or selfish person. They're normal feelings, and you have to deal with them by being strong and mature. HAVING GREAT STUFF DOES NOT AUTOMATICALLY MEAN YOU WILL BE HAPPY. Some extremely wealthy people in the world are very unhappy, despite all they have. Having some things and not others is the situation most people are in. Everyone has to cope with what life has to offer. Nobody has everything, so you just have to face the facts. The old saying "When life gives you lemons, make lemonade" still holds true, as corny as it may sound. When faced with a disadvantage, always give it your best shot to turn it into something worthwhile.

Growing up poor isn't easy, if that's your situation. Everything seems harder. There's no point in blaming anyone—that doesn't help. Feeling sorry for yourself won't do much good, either. It may be a good idea to talk to your family or to an adult at school or to your minister, priest, rabbi, or other religious leader about your situation, so you can understand what the problems are. Sharing your feelings may help boost your confidence.

The best thing you can do is concentrate really well at school, get the best grades you can, and keep moving toward your personal goal to rise above poverty. Education is one important way to create opportunities for yourself. There are scholarships and funding available for all sorts of interests.

If you are old enough to baby-sit or have a job, go for it. Many successful people start at the bottom and work their way up. You have to be willing to work, and you have to keep your eyes open for special opportunities. Ask people in your neighborhood or at school how you can help out. Get involved with a community project. You can even ask family members to join a community activity with you. Be proactive whenever you can.

Go to the school library and read biographies of famous people. Find out how they started out. You may be surprised to learn that many of them had very little when they were young. These people are your inspiration. If you develop confidence in yourself, you can be successful, too. Never let yourself get lazy, and NEVER GIVE UP. As you get older, you'll use everything you learned as a young person to help you visualize the kind of life you want, and you'll be able to make choices for yourself. If you feel trapped in poverty now, remember that time marches on and you will eventually be free to take full control of your own life. It's worth having a great dream, so don't stop dreaming. Believe in your own personal power to have whatever you really want.

If you have a sibling with a physical or mental disability and other kids make fun of you,

the best thing to do may be to talk to them about what it's like for you and your brother or sister. Sometimes kids make fun of others when they don't understand the real situation or have a certain fear about it. Most kids don't really know what it means to have a developmental disability such as autism or some other disability. *You can teach them a lot.* But you have to come from a strong place in your heart in order to teach them. There is no reason for you to feel bad or ashamed about it. Life hands people challenges, and they can be physical, emotional, or even both. Just let go of any shame you feel, like letting a balloon go way up into the sky until you can't see it anymore. Then you can start to give the others important information about your sibling's disability. Just remember that many people in life have disabilities either because of a disease or accident or because they were born with them. What's more, many have loved ones who have disabilities.

Tell the others all about your sibling's struggles and triumphs. Ask your teacher to let you give a report on what life is like with a brother or sister who has a disability. In the report, tell everyone not only what makes it hard for you to deal with but also what makes it an inspiration for you and what you've learned to appreciate because of it. As for kids who still prefer to make fun of you, remember that they are not your true friends anyway. It is better to surround yourself with people who come from love.

If you feel afraid and upset by all the talk about sex, teen pregnancy, AIDS, and abortion,

you are not alone! Many adults find so much about these topics in magazines, on television, on the Internet, and in general conversation to be *too* much. Yes, there is a lot of literature and media focus on the downsides of sex, but they are important issues. People need good, reliable information about them. For someone your age, however, the topics may just seem overwhelming and frightening. Heaps of information can seem difficult to sort out and under-

stand. And a lot of *unreliable* information is out there, too, to make things even more confusing.

The best way to approach this problem is to read material written especially for people your age. Stay away from Internet sites that are meant for adults only (these sites may present material that's unhealthy and troubling for young people). See movies and television shows geared to your age-group. Don't be afraid to talk to adults who care about you. Let them know your feelings about certain topics and why they bother you. One young boy watched a TV show on drug addiction, and afterward he was terrified that he would become a drug addict. He felt so troubled by this that he never shared his feelings until he was much older. Although the TV show seemed to be a horrible experience, he did not become a drug addict. Perhaps if he had spoken to his teacher or someone else about the show right away, he would have saved himself a lot of needless worry.

When you feel upset by the amount of information and all the dramatic stories about these topics, remind yourself that you are strong and smart. You don't have to participate in any activity you know is wrong or harmful. Be your own best friend all the time by telling yourself that bad things do happen to people when they make foolish choices, and sometimes bad things, like sickness, just happen for no apparent reason. No one can avoid all problems. You simply have to deal wisely with them when they arise. And you really can do that. You have an inner power that tells you what is right. All you have to do is quiet your mind, listen, and then begin to help yourself.

If you worry about war, crime, disasters, the homeless, and other disturbing current events,

you may need to stop watching too many news programs on TV or reading news stories in the newspapers and magazines. Everyone is concerned about these unpleasant issues at times. It's normal to have feelings about terrible things that are happening, and it's also fine to want to participate in activities to help alleviate problems. But to dwell on tragedies day in and day out and have them have a bad effect on your personal life is usually unnecessary.

Certain things—like earthquakes or tornados—are nobody's fault. They're called "acts of God." Yes, they can cause great damage and loss of lives, but life must go on. People cope with the damage and rebuild as best they can. Although your concern stems from your being sensitive and sympathetic toward other people's suffering, that concern and worry shouldn't consume your own life.

After a tragedy occurs, the best advice is: *Live your life the way you always did. Do all your normal activities. Don't be afraid to enjoy yourself. Don't stop doing the things you love to do.* Getting on with our lives means that we are strong and capable and that we have personal power, even in the face of an enemy attack or natural disaster. If we all went around scared and depressed all the time, what would our lives be like? If everyone crumbled emotionally, America would crumble. It's your responsibility to take good care of yourself and keep up with your activities and your goals. Although it's fine to be informed about what's happening in the world, it is not fine to let it tear you apart.

Bad things do happen from time to time, and we all have to accept that. To take your mind off death and destruction, listen to your music or do something fun. Try to focus more on all the wonderful things that are going on in the world. Learn more about all the good things people are doing these days—for example, new inventions, new medical advances, and exciting sports competitions. There really is plenty of good news.

Talk to your teachers and your parents about your concerns. Ask them to help you sort out the bad feelings that may not go away so easily. If you wish, ask them to find a group or organization you can join to be an active helper for a particular cause. Actually doing something good can make you feel better emotionally. Remember, life is a gift, and every day is a new day.

If you know someone who tried to commit suicide or who has committed suicide,

you probably feel both frightened and sad. Maybe you even feel angry that such a terrible thing happened. Your feelings are normal.

Suicide—taking one's own life—is very difficult for anyone to truly understand. A person who does not want to live must feel so bad that you can't even imagine it. When someone commits suicide, his or her loved ones are left with all sorts of mixed feelings. They may be devastated, but they may be angry at the same time,

because suicide is the kind of death that can be prevented. It's very different from a death caused by an illness or an accident because the loved one chose to die. That's hard to deal with.

For most people with suicidal feelings, help is available. Someone who is severely depressed can get help from doctors, psychologists, and others, but sometimes nothing helps—for example, if the person is mentally ill. Although the idea of suicide can be very painful for those of us who know that life is really precious, it's important to be strong when things seem to be going wrong and to remember that there's always a way out of pain and troubles if you want to find it.

If you know of a friend or loved one who is thinking about suicide or planning suicide, you can help by telling the adults you trust, even if the person swears you to secrecy. It is not betraying a confidence to tell this kind of "secret," because the person's telling you is actually that person's subconscious way of asking for help. Other clues may be if a person is giving away all his prized possessions or is showing a severe lack of interest in things he used to enjoy.

It's important to be on the lookout for the many signs of depression that are bad enough to make a person consider suicide.

When a young person commits suicide, the people left behind feel even worse about it. They may feel guilty that they didn't realize how bad that person must have felt or what they could have done to prevent such a tragedy. Teenagers who choose to end their lives may not realize that suicide doesn't solve anything. Instead, it wipes out their opportunity to grow up and follow their dreams: They won't have a wedding. They won't have children. They won't be with everyone they love and get to do exciting things. They won't share in the world's unfolding events. And that's incredibly sad.

Where does that leave you? If you know someone who has committed suicide, let that suicide teach you to love yourself better and to say thank-you for everything that's good in your life. Talk to your family and friends about that person and how you can all learn from what happened.

If you think you have suicidal feelings, you may be depressed. Depression is curable! Go for help right away. Don't let bad feelings over-take you. Nothing—NOTHING!—is so bad that it's worth giving up your life over. Tell an adult who cares about you to get you to a psychologist who can help you feel good again. Use your brain, and use the personal power you were born with. You're so worth it!

If you feel tempted to correspond with strangers on the Internet,

please read this section more than once. It is a serious matter that may have serious consequences if you don't use your best judgment.

Stay away from chat rooms in which people are discussing things about sex, violence, crime, or other disturbing subjects. These chat rooms and web sites are not meant for young people. Find topics that are appropriate—that is, *meant*—for your own age-group. NEVER GIVE OUT YOUR REAL NAME, HOME TELE-

PHONE NUMBER, OR YOUR HOME ADDRESS to a stranger who starts to correspond with you. This precaution is to protect you from all the people logged on who may be dangerous. Some people use the Internet to find kids who are willing to talk about disturbing things, meet them in person, and perhaps do them harm. THE INTERNET IS NOT A GAME! It is not a toy! Just because someone is in another state *does not mean he or she cannot find you.* And just because a person may seem very nice and fun online *does not mean that person isn't a child molester or other type of criminal.* Don't be *gullible.* That means don't let people convince you everything's fine when you really can't know that for sure. Be on the safe side and do not identify anything about yourself or your family to a stranger.

Listen to that one more time: *DO NOT IDEN-TIFY ANYTHING ABOUT YOURSELF OR YOUR FAMILY TO A STRANGER ONLINE, NO MATTER WHAT.* For your own protection, do not tell what school you go to, where your mom or dad works, what the names of your brothers and sisters are—none of that information!

Always let your parents know with whom you are corresponding and how you met them. If they don't approve or if they think there might be a problem, you'll have to accept the fact that cutting off from the Internet stranger is for your own good. Lots of young people have been lured into terrible situations by people on the Internet. There have been kidnappings, sexual molestations, and even murders reported that started online between a young person and a stranger. A stranger can be a sexual *predator*. A predator is a person who wants to hunt for someone he can hurt. In the animal world, a tiger may chase a gazelle, catch it and kill it. The tiger, then, is the predator. Got the idea? Adults are not kidding when they tell you not to fool around online.

Use the Internet in a positive way, such as to help you with research for school papers and to correspond with people you know, such as friends and relatives. Steer clear of web sites that are not for young people. Keep your head and your heart free from garbage. You owe that to yourself, because you are smart, capable, and decent and because you have the power to be your own person.

If you feel overwhelmed by peer pressure,

use your head and your personal power. *You do not have to do anything you don't want to do just because other kids want you to do it. Ever.* Stay true to yourself and be strong. For example, if you are being pressured to have sex, your first strategy is not to get into a situation where you have no one to protect you. Don't go to an empty house or any other place alone with someone who may pressure you.

Don't hang out with others who want to

smoke or use drugs or do dangerous things. Avoid what you believe could be trouble. Choose to be with kids who are concerned about the same things you are and also want to avoid problems. You know in your heart there are plenty of ways to have a good time. Doing foolish things won't lead to anything worthwhile.

Understand that peer pressure comes from groups of young people who are trying to be cool, sophisticated, and "grown-up." But when it comes to some of the activities they choose— potentially harmful ones—they lose their cool sophistication pretty fast. And being truly grown-up doesn't have to involve getting the approval of a certain group. Always think for yourself. That's part of having personal power.

You can refuse to be intimidated by peer pressure. If you take the whole picture apart and examine each separate part, you might find that each person in your group would not choose to do some of the group's activities if he or she were alone. Peer pressure often means doing something ONLY IF EVERYONE ELSE IS DOING IT. Although peer pressure is common for young people, if you're a leader rather than a follower, you may be in a better position to deal with the situation. Try to be as independent as you can. You're worth far more than what any group thinks of you, and the smart thing to do is take good care of yourself.

If you want to talk to a counselor but you're worried people will think you're "crazy,"

get real. Psychologists, counselors, and other professionals are trained to help people get through emotional problems. There are very few people in the world who couldn't be helped by talking to a counselor. Everyone has issues to deal with, and many of those issues are unpleasant.

No matter what the problem is, discussing it with a professional may be the best thing you can do for yourself. It doesn't mean you are crazy, or mentally ill, or stupid, or weak. In fact, seeing a counselor or psychologist means you're taking a *proactive* step to help yourself. It means you are willing to admit you have a problem and that you need good advice. That's the first step toward making everything better. Talking to a professional—someone who is not involved in your personal situation—helps you to sort out your feelings and figure out what to do about the problem. It's a smart thing to do.

You can ask at school for an appointment with the school psychologist. Or you can talk it over with your family and have them find a counselor for you. Local religious institutions may offer psychological help and support groups. Also, you should understand that if you don't feel comfortable with a certain counselor, you can ask to see another. Sometimes people just don't "click" with each other. You are better off talking about your problem with someone who makes you feel safe and comfortable. Once you find a counselor you can open up to, you'll find it easier to make progress.

Remember: Good communication can make all the difference!

If you have a crush on someone who doesn't like you,

take time out from your intense feelings to accept the situation. It's okay to feel bad about it. It's tough to be crazy about someone who doesn't care for you in return, and it's sad, too, because in your imagination you'd like to think you and that other person could have such a great time together. If you are certain the other person really doesn't like you, no matter how nice, helpful, or sweet you are to him or her, there's really nothing you can do about it.

But there is something you should know: Crushes happen a lot when you're young. They are a way to recognize what you like in another person and how you get along. All the crushes you will probably experience are like stepping-stones to the relationships you'll have when you're older. You may even have a crush on someone famous, like a rock star or a movie star, or a teacher or a person much older than you. That's normal. Lots of kids have heroes and idols; it's part of growing up. They realize that they can adore someone who is never going to really be a personal friend, and that's okay.

However, sometimes young people can be cruel to each other in matters of the heart. Typically, they show affection to people they like and reject those they don't. They're really trying to be cool and sophisticated—and, like you, they are searching for their own identity and what they find attractive in relationships. One week a girl may be "going steady" with or "seeing" a certain boy, and the next week they break up. Then they turn their attention to other people. You may think the person you have a crush on is the one and only person you'll ever love, but life isn't like that. It is true that some people marry their childhood sweethearts and stay with them forever, but that is rare. Your feelings tend to change as you get older. Everyone's feelings change from time to time. Have more patience for yourself and others in the same boat. Almost everyone you'll ever meet has had a crush on someone who didn't return the feelings. Even if you feel miserable at the moment, you can get over it.

Begin by focusing on someone else with whom you feel comfortable and have a good time. Sometimes the best companion turns out to be a person you already know but never thought of that way before. Maybe someone really likes you in a big way, and you haven't been paying attention! Choose your friends wisely. And get real about friendship. Good relationships require hard work, so give yourself a break and work only on the ones that really count. Someone you thought would be great may turn out to be a rat. Another person you didn't think much of may turn out to be a wonderful friend. Life surprises you with things like this all the time.

Another important thing to remember is that you are young, and you may not really need a steady boyfriend or girlfriend right now. Concentrate on your schoolwork, art, sports, music, or whatever excites you. Friends will show up along the way even if you're not looking for them. And don't forget to *be* a friendly person, the kind of person others want to know.

If you aren't ready to have a boyfriend or girlfriend and other kids make fun of you,

don't worry. First of all, when you *are* ready, things will be different—you'll probably find that you have a special friendship with someone, or you'll know someone you'd like to spend a lot of time with. Being ready applies to many things in life. When you're a baby, you must be ready to crawl and then walk. No one can force a baby to walk if he or she just isn't ready, and no one can say exactly when that will be. Another example is a fruit tree. A peach

ripens in its own time. No one can tell it to ripen faster!

Everyone faces readiness issues at one time or another. People learn at different speeds and in different ways. Some people can learn to speak a second language very quickly and easily, but may have some trouble catching or throwing a ball until they're older. Others may find doing long division and multiplication problems fun and easy, but may not understand much about making a collage in art class or learning the state capitals. One girl may know a boy she likes more than any other boy; another girl may not have any great interest in one particular boy. Or one boy may focus on a girl he thinks is really pretty and smart, whereas another boy has his mind on the next soccer game.

IT'S ALL OKAY! Whatever you choose, it's your life. Stop taking what other kids say so seriously. They are not the authority on young people's relationships! In fact, they are not the authority on any relationships at their age. There is plenty of time to focus on love and friendship during your lifetime, so there's no need to force anything too early. So what if someone makes fun of you because you aren't interested in a special relationship. No one ever said people who have a girlfriend or boyfriend are better than those who don't. That would be ridiculous. There are many people who don't find a love relationship until they're much older, and that's fine, too. Be confident that when you are ready, you will seek a relationship. For now, enjoy everything your life has to offer. Choose your friends and activities wisely and well, and you will be rewarded with many surprises that come from them.

Most of all, be ready to use experience from the past. Be ready to welcome the future, whatever it holds. And be ready for everything that's going on in your life NOW. It's called the *present*, because it really is a gift.

Affirmations

Here are sentences—called affirmations— that can be a gift when you really need a lift. Talk to your spirit: It's a way to talk to the person you are deep down. Pick out your favorite affirmation and say it over and over to yourself. You'd be amazed at how it can help you once it sinks in. Or you can use these as model affirmations to make up your own personal ones. Many adults use affirmations, sort of like short prayers, to get them through a tough situation. Try it. There's a real power in positive thinking, and even more power in the spoken word.

1. I deserve love and kindness.
2. I am an important part of a great universe, and I have a special mission to carry out.
3. Love is the best, sweetest, and most powerful feeling in the world.
4. Love is stronger than anything and always wins out in the end.
5. In my heart and mind, love always has a place, no matter what.
6. When I love someone, my ability to love grows more powerful.
7. It is right and wonderful to love myself exactly the way I am.
8. When I love myself, I can love others.
9. When I love myself and others, I can love the Earth and take care of it well.
10. When I love myself and others, I can love all the animals of the world and receive love back from them.

11. I can make a place in my heart and mind for what I want most, and I trust it will come to me even if I have to wait.
12. Whenever I see something bad going on, I concentrate on the energy and power of love. I send loving thoughts to the bad things so they can begin to disappear.
13. The power in me that is my spirit will live forever, so I am not afraid.
14. I love myself whether I feel happy or sad.
15. I love myself, so I take good care of myself.
16. I listen carefully to the voice of love in my mind and heart that tells me the right things to do.
17. I pray, because prayers are my way of sorting out my problems and talking to God about them.
18. I forgive myself for having bad feelings.
19. I forgive others who have not treated me with kindness.
20. When I forgive, my love grows more powerful.
21. To all the things I think are beautiful in the world, I say thank you for being so

beautiful, even if they can't hear me or understand my words.

22. I count my blessings every day.
23. Love is something you can't see, hear, smell, or touch, but I know it is in me and all around me.
24. I look for signs of love in everyone even if it isn't easy to do so.
25. Love makes everything better.
26. As soon as everyone chooses love, the world will be safer and nicer.
27. Love creates more love.
28. Love is a gift from God no matter what your religious background is or what country you come from. I teach others to love by being kind to them.
29. Love never stops, even when everything seems wrong.
30. When I see another person, I say to myself: "I know you and I are both human. We're not perfect, and we both have our struggles in life."

About the Author

Photograph by Jim Reme

A magna cum laude graduate of Seton Hall University, registered nurse, and former Copley News Service columnist, Tova Navarra has written more than twenty books, including *The Encyclopedia of Asthma and Respiratory Disorders; Allergies A to Z; The Encyclopedia of Vitamins, Minerals and Supplements; Therapeutic Communication; An Insider's Guide to Home Health Care; Wisdom for Caregivers; Toward Painless Writing: A Guide for Health Professionals; Your Body: Highlights of Human Anatomy; The College History Series: Seton Hall University* and *Monmouth University; Images of America: Levittown, the First Fifty Years; The New Jersey Shore: A Vanishing Splendor,* and others. Formerly the art critic and family writer for the *Asbury Park Press,* Ms. Navarra is currently working on an encyclopedia of alternative medicines, a novel, and another self-help book for young people. She is profiled in *Who's Who of American Women,* and she lives in Monmouth County, New Jersey.

Index

Notes to Myself